7 Habits of a HEALTHY, Happy Mom

BY

MONICA BENCOMO

Published in the United States

Design by Divine Enterprises
www.divineenterprisesinc.com

ISBN-13:

978-0615967059 (Monica Martell Bencomo)

ISBN-10: 0615967051

Dedication

I dedicate the hours and resources spent

preparing this book to my son, Eliel R. Bencomo, my

future unborn children, and my husband, Elvis

Bencomo. I LOVE you all!

Table of Contents

Introduction
Tracing the Roots to Unveil the Flower.........................9

Chapter 1
Nurture Your Inner Goddess...................................17

Chapter 2
Body and Wellness—Snatching Your Sexy Back!...................33

Chapter 3
Creating a Detox that Works For You.........................59

Chapter 4
Moms Can Dream Too!..75

Chapter 5
Using Fear as Fuel to Your Advantage.......................89

Chapter 6
Benefits of Being Authentic and Staying True to You......109

Chapter 7
Honor Your Intuition and Abundance Will Follow.........127

Chapter 8
Bringing it All Together to be a Healthy,
Happy Mommy...149

Introduction

TRACING THE ROOTS TO UNVEIL THE FLOWER

My mid-life crisis happened to me around the time I graduated high school. I questioned all of reality, my own intentions and others' officially breaking down in an existential crisis by the time I was 18. Growing desperately tired of my drag, dreary, uninspiring life, I packed up my things at age 20, left Illinois, and moved to Albuquerque, New Mexico with the help of my older sister, Natasha. To say the least, I was *not* on the road to success doing what I had been doing with who I'd been doing nothing with. I needed a change and I needed it fast.

Deciding to reinvent myself, I knew I had to relocate physically in order to allow my inner flower blossom and sprout. Due to all the unpleasant memories associated with my time in Illinois, I felt as though I was trying to grow from concrete—I instinctively knew I had to get nestled in fertile soil to see my best me emerge. Neither my childhood nor my life was anything but perfect leading up to that critical point, but blaming others for my actions made little sense as an adult. I decided to take control and responsibility for my happiness and health—I decided it was time to take control of my life. Looking around in the tiny apartment the freezing winter of 2004 where my "friends" and I lay around gossiping and drinking cheap wine, I promised myself that I would create a better life once and for all. It was as if I kept hearing this voice whispering into my heart, "You don't belong here…" And I'd nod to myself in agreement as if others in the room had heard it too.

Seeds of images were consistently planted in my head and heart inspiring me of my potential future if I could muster up the courage to start over. I kept seeing a better image of myself: Fit, healthy, happy, vibrant skin, discovering my passions and attending to college… transformed from the inside out! Knowing in my heart then that this was all possible despite other's lack of belief in me, I moved forward unapologetically towards my destiny. Needless to say, I never looked back.

What I want to show you, awesome reader, with this book is that once you consciously set your mind to do something (and that something is divinely inspired by a force greater than you), you will be blessed with that gift, and nothing can get in your way *except yourself.* All the things I thought I once wanted that never came into fruition were actually God closing doors *in my favor.* Those once perceived "blocked blessings" were in essence blessings in disguise. The visions we carry for our lives are planted in our hearts from the moment of birth. It is entirely up to us, though, to bring those images forth into reality.

Once I moved to Albuquerque from Illinois and became consciously committed to staying and doing the hard work necessary to transform my life from the inside out, my intuition really began guiding me toward my best life. Some days and nights felt like eternity—there were several times I wanted to pack my things and go back to my old, familiar, yet depressing life in Chicago, but I stayed in New Mexico despite the culture shock and fear of the unknown sensing that there had to be a brighter future in store for me if I did.

I made the changes I knew were inherently necessary for my personal growth I so desperately craved. I ditched the damaging relationships. I stopped seeking love and validation in all the wrong places. I switched from fast foods to whole foods. Physical exercise became a priority in my life. I carved my physique out to *my* best body with discipline and hard work. I landed countless dancing and modeling gigs. In essence, I stopped running from my own potential, and I was rewarded for my efforts: I shortly after met the love and soul mate of my life, Elvis Bencomo, graduated from college with my Liberal Arts degree, and opened up our first restaurant,

Pasión Latin Fusion. My biggest accomplishment of all? Becoming a mommy to my beautiful baby boy, Eliel Ricardo Bencomo. What can I say? Manifestation is real. Life is good. And what we focus on, we create.

I share with you my resume not to impress you, but to bring forth awareness that I **consciously created** my life. Everything I've manifested in my life thus far has been a result of my direct intention. I dream it, and then find a way to create it.

There is no reason you do not deserve to live your dreams. Your dreams are your divine birthright. You own them. You were blessed with innate gifts, and it is your purpose to share them with the world every day. And when you don't, you'll feel discontent unease.

Let this book serve as a reminder to *never settle*. As the awesome motivational speaker Les Brown declares, "You have greatness within you!"

Once I became a mom, a whole new view of life took precedence over the life I had before. I went from planning *my* life to *planning my family's life*. I searched and searched for a book, blog, or community I could truly relate to stay motivated and inspired for women in a similar life predicament. While I did find some great motivation, I sensed I was in a league of my own. And if you are searching for more, you are too. This is what inspired me to write 7 Habits of a Healthy, Happy Mom.

In this book, you will be given all the tools I used to transform my own life for the better. After becoming a mommy, I had to implement some new tools to supplement the ideas which I had already developed to coincide with my new role and lifestyle as a mom. **Beginning this book, you**

will find and notice a lighter-hearted sense, and as you progress, things will get deep! This is because I structured this book as I did with my own journey in life. You start out with the tangible changes that will instantaneously improve not only your outlook, but the entire quality of your life—diet, fitness, lifestyle, organization. The first few chapters are geared towards external changes that will leave you feeling and looking your best from the inside out. As you move forward, you will take it up a notch discovering and fostering dreams for your life, bust through blockages like fear, and learn how to nurture your inherent wisdom and intuition. In order to become genuinely happy and healthy, you must dig both internally and externally to unveil the best version of yourself. These are all necessary steps towards becoming a self-actualized individual and a happy, healthy mom!

Reading each chapter in sequence and **completing the journal-type exercises** following each chapter will undoubtedly lead you down the corridor of fun self-discovery. It is crucial to note that answering your questions thoughtfully and honestly will be immeasurably valuable in your journey.

You have one life to live in your body, with your soul and unique talents in this lifetime. Make a promise to yourself right now that you will commit to this journey and reap the rewards of doing so. And most of all make sure you have *fun* on your journey towards becoming a healthier, happier mommy! This will be an extremely fulfilling process!

Let's begin, shall we?

Chapter 1

NURTURE YOUR INNER GODDESS

That's right, moms. If you want to be the best mom you can be, you must take care of that beautiful goddess staring back at you in your reflection—you! It is not uncommon for women to naturally nurture everyone else in their lives and put themselves last; in fact, society has taught us in subtle and not-so-subtle ways that that is our inherent duty! But I've got a positive newsflash—if you want to be the best mom you can possibly be, paradoxically, you have to make sure *your* most important needs are met first. Why? Because a happy, healthy mama makes for a healthy happy family.

I remember when I first had my son, Eliel—I was so in love with snuggling with him and caring for him (not to mention slightly overwhelmed by the sudden hormonal changes) that I completely neglected myself in the process of adjusting to my new role of motherhood. Afternoon would hit and I would suddenly realize that I hadn't eaten or showered! I've heard of scenarios similar to this by moms all around. Although it is common for many moms to ignore their own needs after having a baby does not make it alright or necessary. With a little practice and positive intention, you can overcome the feeling of guilt that is bound to show up when you take the time to nurture yourself.

In the beginning, I thought that the more I neglected my own "selfish" needs, the better mom and wife I was. Seemingly unable to squeeze in time for showers, exercise, or cooking nutritious meals, the whole day would escape me between diaper changes, breastfeeding, cleaning, and snuggling with my bundle of joy.

When you put everyone else's needs, wants, and desires before your own, you will inevitably end up ill, resentful, and unhealthy in many ways. Neglecting your own body's needs like physical activity, mental stimulation, or having alone time for quiet introspection will rob you of a more joyful existence. When Eliel turned 2 months old, I decided that I was going to change my scattered routine up a bit: I was actually going to make my needs a priority too.

Truth was I not only needed time to cook and bathe, but I also needed time to get out of the house and to connect with other new moms. I joined some mommy clubs and made more friends with similar interests like changing diapers and breastfeeding. It was refreshing to know I wasn't the only new mom in the world. It's so easy to feel so alone in the beginning stages of motherhood. Plus, if you don't make it a point to get outside, both you and your baby can start to get cabin fever. (And that's not good for anybody!)

After joining these mommy clubs I made it a goal to meet women with lifestyles I envisioned myself creating. More specifically, I made a conscious effort to connect with like-minded moms who managed to create envy-worthy lives: A healthy body, a marriage full of romance, happy children and a budding career. *It's possible!* I thought.

Little things we allow ourselves to do can instantly take some of the stress off of our lives. For instance, I would feel badly at times when my house was not spotless with bills paid, errands done, with dinner prepared by 6 P.M. Finally I offered myself some much needed empathy and **gave myself permission** to leave the laundry undone for an extra day or the dishes unwashed for a few extra hours. And low and behold—the chores didn't go anywhere! I was able to pick my chores up from where I'd left them. And when my baby slept, I took the time to nurture my inner goddess—I'd shower, paint my nails, read a spiritually uplifting book, or just plain old relax and sleep myself! After I allowed myself time to just *be*, I instantaneously became a better mom for my boy. And a happy mom makes for a happy baby.

There are so many ways we can cut ourselves some

much needed slack as mothers. If you feel overwhelmed, irritated, or resentful in your life, that is a sure sign that you need to take a moment to be honest about your priorities. What are you doing on your to-do list that you can let go of? What commitments have you made that you may need to politely excuse yourself from? How can you make your life a bit simpler?

Let's go over some practical steps you can take daily to ensure you are not neglecting your inner goddess.

Tips to nurture the motherly goddess in you:

1.   Set boundaries—don't be afraid to say "No!"

When I first had the baby, breastfeeding time was very important to me—it was our skin to skin bonding time. And this may surprise people what with my gregarious nature, but I did not feel comfortable breastfeeding in public or even around family at times. When we received visitors at the hospital after having Eliel, my son, I would politely request time alone with the baby when he needed to feed. For me, breastfeeding felt like such a sacred experience. In my beginning days of motherhood, I wanted to enjoy every special moment with my baby, and at times, I felt I needed privacy. Luckily, my family—both immediate and in-laws—were very understanding.

It was up to me, however, to set those boundaries. Your family and friends may know you, but they are not mind readers. Speaking up and setting personal boundaries will result in radical self-love and respect for yourself as well. **As long as you announce your needs in a respectful way, others should understand**. If not, release the issue to your Higher Power, as you cannot control others' behavior or reactions.

When setting boundaries, it is important here to speak up as quickly as possible. If something doesn't feel right and you've already committed to it, be honest and let the people your decision affects know that you have to decline whatever offer was placed. Saying "No, thank you" will not make you an evil, spiteful woman. Quite the contrary, you will gain respect by others whom wish they could relinquish the need to people please.

Setting boundaries speaks volumes to the Universe. By letting the world know what you need, you are proclaiming **that you deserve to feel light and free—you deserve love!** And often times, we teach others how to treat us by how we treat and value our own selves.

2. *Discipline yourself to sleep at least 7 hours a night*

I know it's hard. My ambitious spirit usually is pulling at me to stay up past midnight *and* wake up before my family. But ladies, if you want to not only feel your best, but look your best—that is, fresh and rested, you must discipline yourself to get that much needed shut eye. When you discipline yourself to sleep 7-8 hours, you wake up the next day not needing an alarm—you are inspired to take on the next day full of natural energy!

Notice that when you do not get sufficient sleep, the snooze button nearly falls off due to your overusing it. Worse off, you don't even get proper rest when you have broken sleep interrupted by the alarm. And to the contrary, when you go to bed at a decent time, you tend to wake up feeling chipper and ready to take on the next day—no alarm needed!

Every time you are tempted to stay up late, gently remind yourself that your inner goddess requires sufficient rest to be her best! We are expected to wear so many hats as mothers—take care of our children, be the maid, the nurse, the chauffeur, the pussycat doll for our husbands—that at this point in my life I can't even imagine doing my daily duties without adequate sleep. Coffee is great in moderation, but it is not a miracle drug. There is no substitute for good ole' shut eye.

3. Have your time to connect with your spirit

Before I begin my day, there's a self-care practice I always make time for: connecting with my Higher Power.

Whether we openly admit it or not, we all often can become depressed, uninspired, or lethargic and have no real reason as to why we should be feeling that way! Our bank accounts are doing alright, kids are healthy, we seem healthy, yet something's just not quite right.

The culprit is probably not your unbalanced hormones or a mid-life crisis. More than likely your soul, spirit, the true essence of who you are has been ignored. And when that happens, all Hell breaks loose.

You can see how making it an intention to spend time nurturing your inner spirit can work magic in your life. You cannot just think positively and expect your negative feelings to just go away. You must allow yourself to delve underneath the surface issues, have quiet introspective time, and let your intuition and your heart guide you towards what you need (more on intuition in Chapter 7).

Having that silence is an essential part of the soul-guided process. All the noise, clutter and violence fed to you daily by the media really can take a toll on your well-being. So instead of waking up and dashing towards the caffeine and energy-sucking program called the News, calm yourself by listening to your inner guidance offer you direction for your day. A subtle shift such as doing this for a few minutes a morning can have miraculous effects in your life. Then you can start living more purposefully with an overflowing joy and everyone around you is going to wonder where it came from.

4. *Treat yourself to a spa day, manicure, date night, or special gift at least once a month*

This, unfortunately, gets overlooked far too often by moms especially. Plagued by guilt of taking time to ourselves, moms tend to allow needs to go un-nourished so that then we can make time to nurturing everyone else's!

I know I am a better mommy when I feel and look my best. When Eliel was first born, I would stare at him in awe—my heart literally overflowing with love, joy, and gratitude for this little boy, and then I'd look in the mirror. My sweat pants from yesterday had spit up on them, my hair looked a hot-mess, and my skin was crying out for an exfoliation. I knew I had to start investing some time in some good-old fashioned self-care while he napped.

You must allow yourself the opportunity to have some much needed goddess time. Don't get me wrong, I absolutely adore the time I get to spend with my son. So much though that I can completely neglect nurturing myself! I'll look around and suddenly realize that my ends have not been trimmed, nails have not been manicured, and that my eyebrows have turned into *one* eyebrow. When this happens, I make a conscious effort to love Monica enough to schedule an appointment at a salon. And when mama gets to provide herself with some much needed R&R, she comes home happier and healthier.   And again—when mama's happy, everyone's happy.

5. *Don't be afraid to ask for help*

This one was hard for me.   I thought I had to prove to everyone that I could do it all when I became a mom.   For some odd reason, I thought I had to be an outright Supermom to prove to other women that it was possible. You know, Supermom—the lady who has 3 kids, is in the best shape of her life, has a booming career, and whose house is spotless *all* the time.

I tried on the Supermom cape a while, and once it dawned on me that this lifestyle was not only impossible, but was a fallacy for other hard-working moms to aspire to, I hung up that cape for good.   I wanted to be inspiring, yes, but deceivingly so? No.

Pushing my ego to this side, I began outsourcing for help. I would call my mom-in-law, my friends, my sister—anyone whom I trusted for some much needed assistance when necessary. It was either that or give up everything else I wanted in life that did not include being a stay at home mom. And my destiny was too important to me to give up on (more on managing your dreams and being a mom in Chapter 4).

I know it can be hard to ask for help at times. As moms we try to do it all and make it look easy, but truth is it's not easy! Being a mom is a full-time career, and it is more than okay to get help when desired. Asking for and seeking help may make you feel vulnerable, but don't confuse vulnerability with weakness. These two feelings live on separate blocks. There is great strength in vulnerability. The saying "It takes a village to raise a child" was created for a reason! Asking Eliel's grandparents to watch him did make me feel a bit vulnerable—sometimes the answer would be no! And who likes rejection? When I need to get some writing or homework done and the grandparents were unavailable, I pay for child-care with someone whom I trust. Taking responsibility for my life makes me feel more confident, at ease, and happy.

Exercises to unveil you inner goddess:

1. What is one way that you can set a much needed boundary in your personal life? (Ex: I often turn my phone off when I need to unwind. This relieves the pressure of feeling like I have to get back to others immediately).

    _____

    _____

    _____

    _____

    _____

    _____

2. When you are tempted to stay up later than you know you should be, what mantra can you tell yourself to encourage you to get some rest? (Ex: When I get enough rest, I am the best me I can be the next day.)

_____

_____

_____

_____

_____

_____

3. What practice would you like to start that will connect you with God, your Higher Power, your soul? (Ex: The first 5 minutes upon waking, you go through all your grateful for before starting your day.)

_____

_____

_____

_____

_____

4. List 3 people you know you can count on to watch your kid(s) while you have some much needed alone time. Taking a step further, call one of these people and

schedule a babysitter so that you can do an activity for yourself. (Even if it is just going to the library and reading for a couple of hours with a hot cup of tea.)

_____

_____

_____

_____

_____

_____

Let's move along towards one of my favorite topics—fitness and health! Obtaining your best body will surely contribute to your health and happiness.

Chapter 2

BODY & WELLNESS: SNATCHING YOUR SEXY BACK!

As we just discussed in the previous chapter, we have to *first* take care of ourselves if we wish to be awesome mommies. Without our own health and strength, we have no energy to share our light with others. And a very large component of our strength is derived from the habits of our health and wellness. If you want to be a healthy, happy mama, you must make exercise and healthy eating a priority in your life.

Before I had my son, I was thin, but not especially strong. I was very active—I'd ride my bike to school, dance in many performances, and even place in 5Ks. Yet, it was after I became a mom that I really took my health and wellness to the next level.

Becoming a mother was the most natural source of inspiration I'd ever been given to propel my health and wellness to the next level. Intuitively, I knew I was the star of not only my own life, but my son's life: I was the person he'd see the most. I wanted to reinvent myself—and quick. I wanted to be the best version of myself so my son would have the best example of what a life of happiness and health looked like. Why wait until the kids are teenagers to set the example of how we should treat our bodies? Although it is never too late to be the person you are meant to be (the best version of yourself), it certainly is never too early either.

With this newfound divine inspiration I had been given after becoming a mommy, I made some radical shifts in my health. I began juicing and gave up the habit of needing to unwind with wine after a stressful day. I greeted each morning with green juice and started to desire processed foods and meat less and less. Water and herbal tea became my favorite drinks. Workouts that challenged me at a new level became increasingly attractive. Sweating became quite the enjoyable activity. And lifting weights suddenly seemed appropriately tantalizing.

Here, it is invaluably important to recognize that like many things in life, **your health is about the journey and not the destination.** Fitness became my friend, not someone I used to get what I want and leave! Far too many times, I see women start a diet in high hopes of losing inches with no compelling reasons *why* they want to become healthier. And what happens when we don't have any compelling reasons for doing something radically different in our lives? We give up and don't stick to the plan only to beat ourselves up for it later. Healthy foods became attractive to me because I wanted natural energy and strength to be an active, happy, vibrant mommy—not necessarily because I wanted to be the hottest mom on the block. I knew I wanted my children to develop habits of health and happiness, so I instinctively knew I had to take them on myself. Practicing what I preached became of the highest importance to me.

There are many benefits when you treat your body like the temple it is including increased energy, confidence, stable moods, and yes—a slimmer figure! My main priority switched after having my son from working out to *look* good to eating healthy and exercising to *feel good*. Looking fabulous was just an added bonus!

Do you ever wonder how others can really commit to healthier lifestyles but you just can't seem to stick to your own? Well, wonder no more. I am here to give you the unfiltered truth as to how you finally can get the health and body you has always desired to feel *and* look your best! Let's begin by clarifying your goals and getting real about your health.

Steps to creating optimal health and wellness:

Step 1: Get real, woman!

Are your expectations realistic? Now, I usually do not advocate using the term 'realistic' when it comes to achieving anything in life, but when it comes to your dream body, I definitely believe a dash of realism can *help* you achieve your fitness goals. Let me offer an example: I do not put any images on my vision boards, Pinterest, etc. unless images are attainable by **my body's standards**. More specifically, I have great legs, but smaller breasts. My body fat percentage went down once I began training for my first fitness competition and the fat in my—guess—boobies went down too! (If you'd like to follow me and see what motivates me on Pinterest, find me here:

http://www.pinterest.com/monicabencomo18/)

So, it'd make little inspirational sense for me to put a woman with a 20 inch waist and triple D's on my vision wall—doing so would only leave me feeling helpless! Investing in $8,000 breast implants is not for me **spiritually** or financially at this point in my life, so I leave said images unpinned, thank you very much. And as a disclaimer: If you decide that getting implants leaves you more fulfilled and is aligned with the woman you're meant to be, kudos! This is a judgment free zone and book. ☺

But you must be real with yourself. You must love the body you were given at birth now so that you can start to reach your own individual potential. We were never all made to look the same, despite the media's persuasive messaging. Never look at someone else's body in envy or jealously. Chances are, they are doing that with others whom they admire and are insecure in their own figure!

Aiming to be a healthier, better you does not have to equate to being discontent or unhappy with where you already are either. I love my body now, but does that mean I need to be complacent and no longer desire growth? No! I want to continue to grow and push my limits and standards. Who knows where refusing to settle can take you?

So, let's get real—how many pounds do you wish to lose? What does the woman of your dreams, the *you* of your dreams look like? Is she curvy in all the right places? Thin and strong? Athletic and toned? The first step in becoming the image of your dreams is to first *decide* what your goals are for your body type. Deciding promotes fertile ground for motivation and *action*.

Step 2: Don't let other's change your vision

Many people, regardless of intention, will try to tell *you* how *you* should look or what you should eat. When I gave up foods that were initially used for comfort or pleasure rather than nourishment, guess what—my weight, of course dropped. Not in an unhealthy way 'I'm starving' kind of way, but just in the 'I'm-off-junk-foods' kind of way. I remember going to dinner with some girlfriends and one exclaimed,

"Oh my goodness, Mo, you've gotten way too skinny!" (Disclaimer: Calling someone "too" anything can be hurtful!) Even though I was only in my early 20's, I knew that I was not "too skinny". I knew I felt my best and that I was feeding my body foods that it needed to function at its best and with vitality.

What's even more interesting is that every woman has what I call her 'ideal weight' and figure—the weight and physique that has her at her best physically and spiritually. For some women, that weight will be 190 pounds, and for other women, that weight may be 120. Your ideal weight will depend on your lifestyle, height, preferred physical activity, and goals. Many women like me are actually more fertile when they lean out! I became pregnant after 3 months of being off birth control (and I'd been on the pill for 9 years prior!). I think my body was able to start ovulating again fairly quickly due to my diet and lifestyle. I was thinner than my average weight when I conceived, but I was healthy. My preferred exercise at that time was walking and running in nature (and cardio always leans me out). I believe that working out in nature helped to restore my balance hormonally which attributed to my ability to conceive. Every woman needs to pay attention to when *she* feels and looks her best. Don't rely on others to inform you of the best version of yourself—that is something only you would know!

To add, there is a "breaking bread" tradition which illustrates that cultures and tribes find it difficult when an individual within that tribe begins to eat for health and nutrition rather than comfort. Dr. Christian Northrup explains that "Breaking bread together is one of the most natural stress relievers on planet Earth". So it can be intimidating to others if you begin taking care of yourself at a new, divinely inspired level. After all, you will be a changed woman! You won't want to hang out late at bars. You won't find pleasure in gossiping for hours over a bottle of wine. And you will no longer sabotage your goals for other's appeasement. But you have got to stay strong, focused, and motivated on the intended goal at hand. Practice what you preach, and you will attract people with similar value systems, and many folks will start to admire you for your determination. Besides, people in your life who genuinely love you will always help support you even if they don't understand your goals.

And, more good news: No one has the power to deprive you of becoming the woman you're meant to be—a healthy, happy mom. You don't need anyone else's approval to shine brightly and to live with healthy standards. Hey, maybe not everyone will *understand* why you are on the path you are on, but it is no one else's duty to. Let me put it a bit more bluntly: Unless it is constructive criticism, people can mind their own business and stay focused on their own divinely inspired goals. (Can I get an Amen?!)

Once you create the image of your best body and are consistently working towards that body, people will come out of the woodwork ready to question you and your goals. "Why do you want to get so muscle-ly?" "You really are skinny, enough" "Why don't you just let men do the weight-lifting?" were just some of the many critiques I was offered in my journey to becoming the best fit version of myself. But needless to say, I did not let the good opinion of others stop me!

Step 3: It's simple; not easy

There will always be some new fad diet out there—some diet that'll make you feel compelled to run out to the health food store and stock up on whatever items you were persuaded to purchase. But you have to be honest—many new diets are ways companies make money off of those whom aren't already disciplined to eat healthy and simply. Thanks to the internet, there is a plethora of valuable information to almost any question we have concerning our health. Doing the research necessary to find out what your body really needs to be functioning at its best is just a few clicks away if not already intrinsically known within you. However, if you just can't seem to stay disciplined to eat what you're supposed to eat (and not eat what you're not supposed to) then you can fall victim by any new, promising, and intelligently crafted advertisement which will seemingly save your day and melt your pounds away with no effort! Next time you see an advertisement for a new diet, smile and change the station. Eating a healthy diet is quite simple: Eat what makes you feel good and avoid the rest.

As an example, I am lactose-intolerant. Over 30 million people over the world are (which makes you wonder if we even need dairy to meet our nutritional needs—turns out we don't)! Ice cream, milk, and excessive cheeses are not my friends to say the least. Yet at times in the past I conveniently ignored this fact because I lacked the discipline in that moment to say no. And while I am a firm believer in cheat meals in moderation, there are ways to cheat that won't upset your digestive system and "clog up you up" so to speak.

My best suggestion for optimum health and wellness is to listen to your body's cues: How do you feel after eating a yummy green salad, full of fruit and leafy greens? Compare that to how you feel after a fast food "meal" and your body will tell you exactly what it prefers.

A diet full of vegetables, fruit, and protein such as beans and grains like quinoa will leave you feeling like a glowing, radiant goddess in no time. Literally, if you try a simple diet similar to this, pounds will melt off your figure at lightning speed. I find that when I am eating clean, I don't have to slave away hours at the gym. When I feed my body nourishing foods created from Earth (and not manufactured in a factory) I only feel the necessity to work out about 3 times a week for 30 minutes. When in doubt as to what you should be eating, refer to these mantras by Kris Carr, author of Crazy Sexy Diet: "If it's made in a laboratory, it takes a laboratory to digest. If it has a shelf life longer than you, don't eat it."

Here's some good news: Our bodies were designed to guide us towards making healthy decisions. We simply have to listen to our body's intuition to know what to eat and when we've had enough. Coupling a simple healthy diet with adequate exercise 3 or more times a week and you'll be one hot mama before you know it!

Step 4: Don't sabotage your sexy!

Whether you realize it or not, the media and the mainstream way of thinking does not exactly perpetuate a 'sexy mother' image. Instead, moms typically are portrayed as nurturing, beautiful beings who sacrifice all their wants and desires for their cubs—including their appearance. And while I am completely nurturing and loving to my baby boy, I do feel that we as moms can (and should) **allow ourselves to feel sexy**. We are divinely feminine—we carried life in our bodies for goodness sake! And how was our bundle of joy created? That's right, through sexy-time…

Thankfully, you do not need to be in the club shaking your romp in order to get your sexy back post-baby. Taking the time to care for your body will inevitably result in a higher libido, and will leave you feeling sexier in your entire wardrobe—no booty-shaking needed!

Before I had my first baby, Eliel, I was a hip-hop/jazz dancer—performing everything from plays to tours to go-go gigs at the club. Feeling like a sexy goddess was no challenge for me at all. Putting on my sparkly costumes, the stage makeup, and high heels would have me feeling like the black and Puerto Rican Marilyn Monroe!

So after I had the baby I sensed that that part of me was gone and would never return—the 'sexy Monica'. And while I *did* hang up my go-go boots for good, I still managed to snatch my sexy back. Between breastfeeding and naps, I would do home workout DVD's and make my healthy smoothies almost every day (my favorite recipes are at the end of this chapter).

The beauty in all this is that I *did not have to wait to feel sexy*! Immediately following a good jog at the gorgeous river "bosque" in Albuquerque, I would drive back home with a huge smile plastered on my face. The natural "happy drug", endorphins, were releasing and I knew I was on my way back to my slimmer figure. Knowing this gave me joy to bask in the accomplishment of taking time to nurture and care for my body which instantly left me feeling like a sexy mama! Realizing that I could enjoy the journey and not be in a rush to the destination was a big relief.

The best part of it all was that I lost all 40 pounds of my pregnancy weight at home or out and about in nature with my son—no gym needed. My favorite gym did not accept children under 8 months of age, so I invested in some valuable home workouts and got creative with exercises I could do out in nature with my baby and a stroller (my postpartum workouts are all available on my Youtube.com/MonicaBencomo).

Working towards your fitness goals and staying true to who you are in the process will serve you in feeling more confident, sexy, and fulfilled immediately. Staying focused on your daily tasks at hand, i.e. yoga *today*, 1 mile jog *today*, will help you to enjoy the process because you'll know you are living and leading a healthy, inspiring life!

Exercises to unveil your inner goddess:

1. What do you look and feel like at your healthiest? What would your body look like if it reaches its highest potential? (Ex: When I stick to a healthier lifestyle, my skin is vibrant, I am about 145 pounds, and I am full of energy!)

    _____

    _____

    _____

    _____

_____

_____

2. List at least 2 compelling reasons why you are willing to
    take your health to the next level. For me, my son was
    the prevailing factor here. I wanted to set the example
    for him. (Another example would be a mantra such as, "I
    deserve the best nutrition for my body because I love my
    body!)

    _____

    _____

    _____

    _____

    _____

    _____

3. What are some simple action steps you can take today
    that will lead you towards a healthier lifestyle? (Ex: Throw
    away the ice cream in the freezer. Donate the processed

foods in the cabinets to a homeless shelter. Go stock up on fresh fruits, vegetables, and proteins.)

_____

_____

_____

_____

_____

4. How can you feel sexier today? (Ex: Instead of wearing the raggedy t-shirt to bed, I will surprise my man with a brand new pair of booty shorts. I will put on red lipstick, just because it is Tuesday. I will wear a pair of my sexy heels today and save the flats for tomorrow.)

_____

_____

_____

_____

_____

_____

5. Create a workout schedule and commit. There's a saying—"Failing to plan is planning to fail." Creating a plan will result in higher productivity and will further help establish new, healthier habits. Enough's enough—no more waiting for the perfect time. If you want to join the gym-do that! If you prefer a home workout—purchase a dvd today or head to my Youtube.com/MonicaBencomo to view some of my free fitness videos.

Monday:_____

Tuesday:_____

Wednesday:_____

Thursday:_____

Friday:_____

Saturday:_____

Sunday:_____

Monica's Fitness Guide to Feeling and Looking Her Best!

Monday: 15 Minute Leg Circuit + 10 Minutes Cardio

Tuesday: 15 Minute Upper Body

Wednesday: 20-30 Minute jog outside with Eliel

Thursday: 10 Minutes Abs

Friday: Cardio of choice

Saturday: Off—walk optional

Sunday: Family walk—no time restraints

ADDED BONUS:
MY TYPICAL DAILY DIET

- Full bottle of water with lemon and glass of green juice first thing in the morning

- Breakfast: One of my morning smoothie recipes listed on **page 57**

- Lunch: 2 slices Ezekiel bread with avocado or almond butter

- Snack: Green juice + smoothie

- Dinner: Quinoa and vegetables

- Before bed: Herbal tea

- Late night snack if hungry: almonds

- **Be sure to take a multivitamin daily before bed to help restore nutrients in the body while you sleep. Also, take an Omega 3 if you do not put flaxseeds in your smoothies.

There you go. When you put your goals down on paper, it has a way of motivating you in ways you cannot articulate or see. So make a plan! You can always tweak it as you go.

On the following pages, please find my favorite smoothie recipes. My weight shed so easily postpartum due to drinking these smoothies. Even though I was breastfeeding, my caloric and nutritional needs were still being met. I would make two smoothies a day as meal replacements (plus the other meals listed) and my caloric intake was still between 1500-1800 calories! *The best part is that I saved so much time with cooking.* My son's diet consisted only of milk for his first 5 months of life, and I kept my supply and energy up by feeding my body fruits, veggies, and protein. I didn't have to stress out by trying to cook every day.

Today, I still use smoothies as 50% of my diet. Drinking my food the first half of the day saves me time, and I feel great because I know I am eating the nutrients my body needs. Try some of the recipes and don't be afraid to tweak it to your personal taste.

SMOOTHIE RECIPES

These smoothies can be an entire meal replacement. Recipes serve 2-3. Feel free to store for later (up to 2 days in mason jar). Ingredients listed in order added to blender.

MO'S GREEN SMOOTHIE DELIGHT:

- 1 cup water
- 1 cup unsweetened almond milk
- 2 cups frozen fruit
- ½ banana
- 2 cups spinach
- 2 tablespoons of Greek yogurt

PERFECT GREEN PROTEIN SMOOTHIE:

- 1 cup Water
- ½ cup unsweetened almond milk
- 2 cups frozen mixed fruit
- 2 cups spinach
- 1 scoop whey protein
- ½ Banana

TROPICAL SUMMER SMOOTHIE:

- 1 cup water
- 1 cup coconut milk
- 1 banana
- 1 cup frozen mango
- 2 tablespoons Greek yogurt
- 2 tablespoons flaxseeds
- 1 teaspoon of honey

GREEN PARADISE:

- 1 cup water
- 1 cup (no sugar added) juice of choice
- 1 cup frozen broccoli
- 1 cup spinach
- 1 cup kale
- 1 banana
- 1 cups frozen fruit

MORNING ENERGY:

- 1 cup water
- 1 cup coconut milk
- 2 tablespoons almond butter
- ½ cup dry oatmeal
- 1 cup spinach
- 1 cup fruit

Bonus: My go-to green juice recipe:

GLOWING GODDESS GREEN JUICE:

- 4 cups kale
- 1 lemon
- 1 inch ginger root
- 1 green apple
- 1 cucumber

Congrats! You are on your way to feeling gorgeous from the inside out! Let's move right along to creating your own detox that works for your schedule, needs, and desires.

Chapter 3

CREATING A DETOX THAT WORKS FOR YOU

Have you ever thought of creating your own detox—a detox plan that is congruent with *your* personal goals and intentions in life? On this journey to becoming a fit, healthy, and happy mom, you may be interested in a faster pace towards optimum health and wellness. If this sounds like you, a detox plan may be just what the doctor ordered. Detoxing is a fabulous way to cleanse your body of built up impurities and toxins.   All the late-night brownie binges, alcohol, coffee, and breads can really start to clog up your precious system. Committing to a detox program is a surefire way to jumpstart your vitality.

Before you start creating your own detox, let's first define what a detox entails. We've all heard the term, but do we really understand the meaning? The type of detox that I am referring to in this book is a process one gets very specific on what she wishes to feed her body *and* spirit for a specific amount of time. Interestingly enough my definition of a detox refers to what you allow into your space, your body, and your spirit.

Many begin a detox solely in hopes of shedding those last few annoying pounds, clearing skin, or to fit into their wedding gown. But I created my first authentic detox because I was spiritually hungry for much more than met the eye.

I was hungry for an internal transformation. My soul was ready to evolve, yet everyone in my life was comfortable with the older version of me which I was ready to shed. What beginning my detox meant for me was that certain folks I hung around, certain substances I allowed into my body, and some engagements previously made had to be cancelled in order for my **new me** to emerge. I believe our lives drastically improve if we are willing to make the necessary changes to better ourselves. It was as if my intuition kept whispering: "If you let go of all that is not serving you and commit to a higher way of being, you will have the life of your dreams and it will be for the highest good of all." So, I obliged!

But hey, no one said it was going to be easy.

Why would anyone consciously want to forgo their earthly desires such as sweets, alcohol, and deep-fried chicken wings for a certain length of time? These things bring great joy!

However, an even better question here would be *why not?* Why wouldn't you be willing to let go of items that clog up your arteries, drain your energy, and pack on the pounds? The mainstream way of living will tell you that you *deserve* to feed your body crap because hey—*you work hard! You deserve the late night pizza and beer!* Yet, when you are working hard and expecting your body to be the vehicle for your daily life and function efficiently, feeding your body nutrient deprived foods should not be viewed as a *treat*. I'm going to be bold enough here to say that I think you deserve better. What your body really deserves are nourishing products that naturally support and sustain your energy levels.

I don't know about you, but if I have had a long day and I am exhausted, the last thing I want is to give more of is my energy to try and digest foods that aren't easily digestible. Instead, I practice one of the self-care habits we talked about in Chapter 1. Feeding my body things like green juice or a green smoothie when I think I need another coffee is one of the many ways I honor my body's wisdom and naturally maintain my energy levels.

When I really buckled down and started my journey of my first detox, I didn't tell much anyone else except the church I'd been frequenting and my husband. I wrote all my goals in my journal: I wanted to take my life to the next level. I wanted to attract more friends who matched my energetic vibration. I wanted to feel less easily agitated and more peaceful.

My detoxes have always helped me reach my divinely inspired goals. Now, I will share with you my personal tips on how to create your own successful detox pertaining to your own lifestyle and personal goals you wish to achieve.

Let's start off with the tangibles—food, drink, and what you should be avoiding in these categories overall in *any* detox. With your detox, you should be monitoring what you feed your physical body. Here is a list I've compiled which include the overall **no-no's** when beginning a detox:

1. Alcohol

2. Junk foods

3. Processed foods

4. Excessive caffeine

5. Dairy products

6. Overall, anything detrimental to your health and well-being

Now, let's go over the things you **should be** consuming while on any healthy detox:

1. Plenty of water (*at least* 2 liters a day)

2. Fruits

3. LOTS of vegetables

4. Herbal tea

5. Optional: proteins such as beans, legumes, or nuts

6. Overall, more items made from Mother Earth, less items made in a factory.

As I mentioned, an authentic detox can also mean **letting go** of other things which are detrimental to your well-being such as:

1. Rude behavior (There are healthy ways to vent frustration like talking with someone you trust or going for a jog.)

2. Excessive negative thinking (Develop positive affirmations to counteract negative beliefs you may have.)

3. Jealousy and possessiveness

4. Relentless Anger

5. Being unwilling to forgive

6. Inauthentic company

7. Overconsumption of media—T.V. phones, or social media

8. Negative nay-sayers

9. Overall, anyone or anything in your life which is no longer serving the person you wish to become.

An added note: once you've committed to your detox and really clean up your eating habits, all sorts of unresolved issues can creep up. This is because we often use food as a source of comfort and love when we are lacking peace at times. So when you have something come up—anger, frustration, impatience—become aware of the desire to cover these emotions up with food. By shining light on the dark emotions, you will gain strength to make conscious decisions concerning your health and happiness. Committing to a life with less and less toxic foods and distraction may not be easy, but it will be worth it.

Aside from cleaning up your diet, contacts, and emotional baggage, a healthy detox will also include de-cluttering your space! My home is not a mansion, but it is peaceful and clean. Friends often come over and ask me to help them organize their own home. This is because you see space, cleanliness, and order when you walk into my apartment. I released anything I no longer needed and that no longer served me by donating many of our possessions that no longer served our family. Your inside world will always be reflected back to you. If you feel a hot, distorted mess on the inside, don't be surprised if your house is always a mess. Detox your home as well so you can be on the highway towards feeling some inner contentment. Here are some helpful tips to assist you along the way:

Tips to detox your living space

- Go through your closet and donate all your clothing that does not make you feel beautiful

- Organize that junk drawer

- Sort out bills and shred old papers that you know you really don't need

- Sign up for paperless billing to save some tree

- Sell anything that is still of high value that you no longer need on Craigslist

- Donate the rest.

Now, let's go over the **duration** of a detox. This is going to depend on the goals of the individual. For instance, I did not consume any alcohol during my 21 day cleanse, yet, I did not swear off a good glass of wine for life. Also, the stricter any detox is, the less of a time constraint I would put on it. Ask your inner guidance what you need to release from your life. Some big ones would be: Cigarettes, drugs of any kind, alcohol, junk food, and excessive sweets such as cakes and cookies. Everyone is different, yet everyone has their own vice. Knowing what your addictions are and being honest about telling yourself will be very helpful in this process.

What you may come to find in your detox is that you swear off cigarettes or sweets for two weeks and you wake up the 15th day not craving them. And that my friend, is when you should treat yourself to a lovely pedicure and *not* a cupcake! That means you will have conquered your addiction and freed yourself from its cage!

Every goddess needs to detox a couple times a year. I've committed to completing a detox once a quarter, or once every season. It is an impactful yet simple way to check in and ensure I don't have any unhealthy or non-serving addictions robbing me of a more fulfilling life subconsciously.

Warning: many people along your journey may become uncomfortable at your body and soul's progress during your detox. Greatness always encounters opposition! Instead of condemning or becoming judgmental on other's actions in lieu of your own personal growth, vow to remain humble and lead by example. Think about it: 5 or 10 years ago, would the younger version of yourself want to hang out with the woman you've blossomed into today? Would you understand her actions and desires? Most likely, the answer to that is no. She probably would have intimidated you!

Remember the saying 'birds of a feather flock together'? Well, like attracts like, and we usually prefer others whom are on our energetic wavelength, so to speak. This is because we are all on our own path going or growing at our own speed. Life is not a race, but that doesn't mean you are meant to take the scenic route either. Know in your heart why you are committing to a cleaner, simpler way of life, and know that you will be blessed infinitely for living more consciously. And trust me, before you know it, your inboxes, voicemails and doorstep will be filled with people wanting to be in your presence. "Something's different about you…" they'll say with a smile. And you'll know why, and that's all that is important.

Exercise: Detox Your Way to the Life of Your Dreams:

1. What items do you consume or allow into your body that you are sick and tired of? What do you wish you had more direct control over? (Ex: Too many chips after work? Too much coffee during the day? Be open.)

   _____

   _____

   _____

   _____

   _____

   _____

2. Are there any people, commitments, or things your intuition has been leading you away from? (Ex: Is your best friend willing to grow *with* you or do you feel held back? Do you have anyone in your life that you feel may be sabotaging your goals towards becoming a better you?)

_____

_____

_____

_____

_____

_____

3. Why do you feel your inner guidance is urging you to break free of this or these addictions, even if temporary?

_____

_____

_____

_____

_____

_____

4. What can you donate in your home that is no longer serving you?   Make an appointment to have it/those items picked up immediately.

_____

_____

_____

_____

_____

_____

5. How do you expect to feel upon completing your _____
   day cleanse?

_____

_____

_____

_____

_____

6. Now, the logistics of your detox challenge:

   - When do you plan on starting?

   _____

- What are the items you wish to focus on consuming?

_____

_____

_____

_____

_____

_____

- What items are you focusing on avoiding?

_____

_____

_____

_____

Congratulations, friend! You are on your way! Doesn't it already feel freeing and exuberating? I instantaneously felt freer when I first began this journey and donated my TV, much of my clothing, and other items. If living simply and authentically sounds good to you, then get ready to feel the most free you've felt in a while!

Chapter 4

MOMS CAN DREAM TOO!

Is it just me, or is there some unwritten code or contract out there stating that once you have a baby, you have to hang up your dreams too? I highly doubt it's just me due to the fact that the hundreds of women I've spoken to at workshops, coached, or friends have all agreed to sign this verbal contract both consciously and subconsciously. Their hearts nag with indecision: I really want to have a baby (or another baby), but is it the right time? Will I become one of those women who wear mom pants and flats every day, never again sharing my gifts other than motherhood with the world? I've got great news: Of course not! And refer to my blog MomsWear*Heels*.com for further evidence!

First off, I am a huge proponent of having it all. But I do couple this idea with a disclaimer: we all define having it all and being successful quite differently. To further add, we can have it all, just not all at once!

I'll illustrate this with an example: After being married for 5 years, I caught baby fever like an incessant yet pleasant plague; nothing I could do would get the image of me pregnant or cooing a baby out of my mind. My heart was craving this new chapter, yet my head wasn't on the same page: *What if I never dance again? Will freedom become a thing of the past? Can I still live purposefully towards my goals and destiny?* Illegitimate worries and concerns flooded my mind. And in retrospect, of course I will and I have continued to do my passions since becoming a mommy. But back then my head would conjure up some of the most defeating images to try and force my heart down from winning.

But you can only ignore your heart's calling for so long. Before I knew it, I was prancing around with a big ole' belly happy as can be and soon after that breastfeeding my new bundle of joy! And while I could not go out drinking with my friends, accept any offered dance gigs, or toast at my sister's wedding during my pregnancy, *I was joyful and content.* I knew my intuition was leading me down the path best fit for me. My heart was overflowing with joy. And I knew I'd made the right decision.

My first year of motherhood was an amazing one. I learned so much more about me, my husband, and of course our baby in this time. Allowing myself the liberty to enjoy my time with my little one, I drastically cut my hours at work and school and gave Eliel the majority of my energy. Gladly, I can honestly say that I don't have any regrets! And after much patience and diligence with being a stay at home mommy, my heart felt ready to go after another aspect of my destiny: fitness, life coaching, and inspiring women's lives on a different level!

Your heart will never guide you wrong. Your heart will always have the best intentions for your life in mind. In your heart you can find clues to the steps needed to be taken towards realizing your destiny. All you need to really do is stay open and receptive to your higher guidance. As women, moms, daughters and aunties, our intuition was inherently given to us upon birth. We just need to practice listening to our wisdom more often, and **cease doubting its inherently wise nature.**

I believe you sometimes need to keep certain goals towards your destiny a secret. If you go around sharing your visions of your life with those around you, even if they love you they may not understand. This is because intuition is an illogical inner GPS system that **only you know** how to function. And in an effort to protect you from making an illogical decision which others may be unable to comprehend, they will warn you against following your dreams. This is mainly due to society's way of glorifying *methodical* GPS systems. But honoring your logic and mind over your heart and soul will end up with you losing the game of life and will make you anything *but* healthy and happy. Even according to

Dr. Christiane Northrup M.D., "When there is a conflict between the intellect (what we think) and the heart (what we feel), the heart ALWAYS wins. But sometimes the feelings of the heart become translated into symptoms or illness so that we are forced to stop and feel them fully."

Do yourself a favor—listen to and respect what your heart is telling you to do. By honoring your intuition, you will be led towards a life full of purpose, passion, and pleasure!

Tips to help you dream big...even if you are a busy mama!

1. **Look within** to discover your heart's calling. Perhaps you already were aware of your purpose prior to becoming a mom—in this case; you are one of the lucky ones! If you are like the majority of us whom are still open to discovering our true purpose (other than being amazing nurturers) then this step is for you: **Create a vision board.** If you already have one, update it. This can be a great activity for you and your whole family! A

vision board is a simple, yet effective tool that can help anyone manifest their most authentic desires. And it's a creative yet easy process! (If you've never made a vision board—no worries. There is additional info about vision boards below in the workbook section.) Just ensure your board of inspiration is somewhere of high visibility. Which room do you frequent the most at home? Put it there. If you are a more private person, keep it in your bedroom, private bath, or office. No one needs to be in your personal business if that is not your desire!

2. **Pray for guidance.** I promise—we are not the most intelligent forces in the Universe. Praying to your Higher Power, however you choose to name this Force, will serve you in making better decisions. Your intuition will always know what is best for you even when the guidance seems illogical. In the past I've prayed about the next route I should take concerning the path for my family or career and at times, my inner guidance responded ever so

clearly, yet not with the answer I was hoping for or expecting. In this case, obedience has always been necessary to help propel me to the next level of my life. Knowing that I do not know what is best for me logically and that my heart is many times more powerfully intelligent than my head, I've made it a habit to surrender to my Higher Guidance.

3. **Go for it!** Once your vision board is complete and you are clear more or less on what you wish to do to feel good about your life, make some plans, woman! Your heart can be full of well-meaning desires, but if these intentions are not manifested into reality, then you've wasted your gifts and that would be a tragedy. I believe that one of the saddest experiences in human history is to feel full of regrets and be nearing the end of your life. Don't let this be you! It may be helpful to even meditate on this a bit: When I pray for further understanding or clarity concerning a decision I have to make, I often

conjure up an image of myself when I'm about 80 years old. I inquire: *Is this something you would have me do? Is this something you will regret if I do not do?* And if the answer is a resounding 'yes', I move forward with confidence.

4. **Double check your motives.** If you truly wish to live an abundant, joyful life, you must ensure you are not living based off selfish intentions. If your goals are only appeasing to you, where is the service in that? I believe we are all on this earth to share our God-given gifts and talents. Doing so is being of authentic service. Yet, if you set a goal and only envision your own material success, popularity, and respect of others, you will end up only in disappointment. Why is this? Well, when we are doing what we truly love and enjoy, we are of highest service because we are sharing our passion and enthusiasm with the world. If we, on the other hand, apply for a job or do something not because we are drawn to it, but rather to gain envy of others, we are ignoring a higher will for our

lives. I don't know about you, but I fully trust the vision given to me for my life. This fact makes it easy for me to submit my will, release selfish ambition, and make decisions based off the highest good of all.

5. **Give yourself permission to want what you want.** Once you know your motives are clean and the desires in your heart were put there by a Higher Power and not your ego, move ahead with confidence and grace! When this is the case, your path will be protected. Do not apologize for your authentic desires, go after them with certainty! If you share your vision anyone in your life, and you hear negative feedback, fret not. Once you are on the path you are meant to be on, those aligned with your destiny will suddenly show up, and with perfect timing. Also, something else I've learned along my journey: Good friends will never be intimidated by your success; in fact, *they will be moved by it.* Those meant to

share your journey will become inspired and spiritually fed by witnessing your live and manifest your dreams.

In short, nurture the dreams you have for yourself. Having baby does not equate to releasing or letting go of your destiny!

Exercise: *Dream big, mom!*

1)   Throw a vision board party either for you and friends or you and your family. What are some goals that meet the criteria listed above? Become clear on that first by listing a few personal goals for yourself this year. (Examples: Go back to college. Fall in love. Have a baby. Go on vacation. Write a book.) The opportunities are endless. Next, create your vision board and materialize your mental dream images. Instructions on creating a vision board are below. Have fun! This is an exciting process.

_____

_____

_____

_____

_____

_____

_____

_____

- Collect a blank poster board, glue stick, scissors and at least 5-10 magazines

- Go through the magazines, cutting out *anything* that inspires you (You do not need to know why something is inspiring yet. It can be words, phrases, images—you get the idea).

- Collect your images. Arrange them on your board as you feel appropriate. Get creative!

2) Write at least one thing you can do right now towards one of the goals on your list. (Example: purchase a domain name for your blog you'd like to start or sign up for a 5K.)

_____

_____

_____

_____

_____

_____

3) Do you believe pursuing and accomplishing your goals will serve a purpose higher than selfish ambition? Why or why not? Be specific.

_____

_____

_____

_____

_____

_____

4) How do *you* define success?

_____

_____

_____

_____

_____

_____

Alright, mama, you are on your way towards radical self-actualization! Let's move right along to the discussion on fear: a speed hump that may bump you up from time to time towards creating a happier, healthier life and how you can prepare yourself not to get paralyzed by it.

Chapter 5

USING FEAR AS FUEL TO YOUR ADVANTAGE

An essential ingredient for an amazing life as a mommy will definitely include going after your dreams. And once you decide what those dreams are, and are on your journey towards becoming a healthy, happy mama, there is one emotion that is sure to come nagging at you other than sheer inspiration: fear. This is because fear of change is one of the most frightening emotions we all experience universally. And on this journey, you *will* be making some radical changes to your life.

Fear is a completely natural emotion. Although it is

bound to show up while you are on the journey toward

becoming the person you are meant to be, you *can* push past

it.

Let's look at fear metaphorically for a moment:

Imagine you are on a starting line about to begin the race

called 'life'. This starting line is painted into on the floor

bright yellow. You want to cross the finish line just to begin

the race! But fear whispers in your ears—*you can't start! You're*

not good enough! You will fall; you will fumble! It's best to stay here,

behind the starting line. Here, you are comfortable! Let's play it safe—

stay here, with me.

But this is not the voice of intuition or love. This is

the voice that is stopping you from escaping the *mental prison*

of complacency. This is the voice that doesn't believe in you.

And although fear is just an illusion—a line drawn on the floor of your consciousness—it can be a powerful one nonetheless and can separate you from taking your life to the next level. But there's great news—you don't have to let this voice win. You can develop tools necessary to slap that sucker right out of the way so you can be free to run towards a happy and abundant life for you and your family.

Have you ever wanted to do something but talked yourself out of it due to lack of confidence and fear of the unknown? When I first really gave myself permission to want what I wanted a while back—a baby—all types of crazy, illogical thoughts ran through my mind. From 'I'm too young' to 'I'm too irresponsible', I scared myself away from getting off the pill several times even though my life's resume looked pretty good: I'd been married for 5 years, was a successful business owner, college graduate (take that irresponsibility!), and was 26 years old. Finally, I faced my fears of "not being ready" and decided to have a baby!

That was one of the best decisions I'd ever made. Having my son enriched my life in ways I cannot even begin to articulate. And what if I'd allowed fear to stop me in my tracks? I wouldn't be reaping the benefits from *facing* them.

But fear will rear its head again and again in your life. This is why you must prepare and armor yourself with the appropriate tools when fear shows up at the door of your dreams. Even after I became a mom, a life coach, and business owner—before I buckled down to write this book, my fear took the disguise as my ego. My ego pleaded, *"What are you doing? You can't tell people your insecurities! You can't tell them about your past! They won't respect or admire you!"* You see, fear was making me believe that in order to be loved I had to protect my precious self-image and appear flawless since birth in order to be inspiring. My ego wanted me to keep pretending like I had it all together since the beginning of time. But there is one thing I know for sure and that is this: You attract **authentic success** when you build your life and dreams based off of your authentic *self.* I didn't want to be liked, respected, or admired for fractured pieces of who I was: I want to inspire by telling women the truth of the big picture—not just the all that glittered with gold.

I have since learned to have fun with this evil voice called 'fear' in my head. Truly uncaring of how crazy I must appear, I outright engage in a conversation with this beast! I flat out yell aloud where Mr. Fear can stick himself when his energy attempts to drag me away from my dreams—(hint: It's where the sun don't shine).

How many of you can relate to this? How many times have you *talked yourself out of something you knew you should be doing due to this unworthy voice in your head?* Far too many of us, I'm sure. An amazing moment came to me when I realized that fear could be used as *fuel* to propel me into the unknown; the future I had not yet seen. I realized I had to develop *tools of courage* that I could use consistently, or I'd despise myself later for not going after what I truly wanted.

A simple method I use to catapult me into taking action when I am afraid is fast forwarding my life. I imagine myself a very much older woman; only this version of me didn't do the things I knew I was meant to do. This woman is full of wisdom at her old age, only it is too late —she is already on her death bed. She looks at me intensely and urges, "You've got to do the things you know you ought to do! If you don't, you'll end up like me; full of nothing but regrets and "should-as". You only have one body, one life on this Earth—do the things your heart yearns to do!" And then she fades away, and I'm brought back into reality. I ask myself, "If I don't do this, how will I suffer?" Gratitude fills me as I thank my Higher Power that I still have the time and opportunity to live my dreams.

Shortly after I graduated from college with my Liberal Arts Degree, I was let go from my secretarial position I had been working. I was a work study, and had been in the Human Resources Department at my college for over a year. I remember my boss pulling me over to the side with a blatant look of apology on his face. My boss Jesse informed me with a sincere look of pity that he had to let me go since I was no longer enrolled in full time courses due to my graduating. I wanted to smile and thank him, but I refrained—little did he know, I was quite relieved! I hadn't the courage to quit previously due to familiarity —I had what I call the "being comfortable syndrome". I felt as if he'd *released me to find my true calling.* Even if I didn't know what my true calling was at the time, I knew I was much more likely to find my purpose now given the time I'd save not having to file hundreds of papers.

I smiled as I walked out of those HR doors towards the unknown. I knew I needed to find a new job, yes, but my husband was working full time as a chef, so I didn't feel intense pressure of having to find a job right then and there.

Shortly after I was released from my secretarial position, my husband, Elvis, pulled me to the side one morning while doing my hair to inform me of a potential new business venture. His co-worker let him know of a new restaurant space coming available for lease that summer. Elvis asked if I thought we should look into it. "Sure, why not?" I said as I curled my hair. I wondered what we had to lose and decided that was nothing.

A week or so later we saw the restaurant in person. Next thing I know, we're finding an investor, signing a lease, and remodeling the place. And then all of a sudden one day while painting our new restaurant it hit me like a ton of bricks— we're going to be restaurant entrepreneurs—eeek!—this is scary! I realized we no longer would have the cushion of a solid bi-weekly income. I called my close confidants in tears asking for advice that I hoped would give me strength. Instead, I was greeted with empathetic feelings matched with scary, realistic statistics—"More than 90% of restaurants fail within the first year; I understand why you're afraid!" *Thanks,* I thought sarcastically. That's exactly what I needed to hear *after* signing the lease.

I literally experienced anxiety attacks due to my fear of opening our own business. I believed in my husband and his dreams; don't get me wrong—I knew of his amazing talent in the kitchen. I just felt overwhelmed. Having your own business is like having a child. It requires intense, consistent attention paid to it in order to keep it functioning properly. I wondered if I had the strength, knowledge, tenacity, and discipline required to be self-employed. I decided that answer had to be yes—that there was no other option—the anchor had already been released and my boat was taking off. I decided to be faithful—the Universe had been guiding us the whole time in our journey of becoming young business owners and I hadn't even noticed! Everything had come together so effortlessly that it seemed like divine intervention. Obtaining the several business licenses, negotiating the lease, hiring help—everything was flowing and we were learning at an incredibly fast speed as we went along. In retrospect I see that Elvis and I had it in us to move forward the whole time; I just conveniently ignored this fact due to a nagging sense of fear. All of a sudden with this realization, I had tremendous confidence—we *can* do this! The mental weight of the risk no longer held me down. I felt free to move forward.

Have you ever known you were meant to do something with your life but just lacked the faith necessary to propel you forward to combat fear?   I certainly have.

Becoming aware of this, I developed a simple tool to aid me

in moving forward in my life with confidence: When my faith

and trust in the higher vision for my life wavers, I borrow

some. I wish I had unwavering faith 100% of the time, but

until I get there, I will borrow it from those I feel can afford

to give some away. I'll never forget the moment I was

experiencing insecurities in my writing this book. I stumbled

across a video one morning while on YouTube searching for

some inspiration. A video of Lisa Nichols at Awesomeness

Fest caught my attention. Lisa stated in a powerfully

compelling voice: "Have blind, unwavering, unapologetic

faith in who you are destined to be, and on the days when

your faith wavers, borrow mine."—how beautifully giving of

her! It was as if my intuition knew exactly what I needed to hear to continue on my journey towards discovering my purpose—it was as if I was guided directly to Lisa at the most opportune and appropriate time to help me move forward in my life's purpose.

Lisa Nichols helped me realize why we all can benefit from mentors and coaches in life. These are the strong in which we can borrow faith from when we feel weak. All of my mentors I look up to most—I haven't even met yet. Relying on the internet, books, and videos I create the connection between them and me to help foster a sense of genuine community. I have a list of authentically genuine individuals I go to when I feel doubtful or insecure—some of them are Lisa Nichols, Oprah, Les Brown, Maya Angelou, Martin Luther King, Gandhi, Dr. Christiane Northrup and so many more. They all represent strength, confidence, vulnerability, and divinity in their own special way and I passionately respect those qualities. They also all had *compelling reasons* for pursuing their goals in life. When your reasons for going after something in life are truly meaningful and impactful, fear gets knocked off to the side. And remember: Your mentors don't always have to be tangible, or even living. These people simply must speak to your own heart in a way that is so inspiring that it gives you strength to move forward when feeling stuck.

The main mentor or life coach I go to, though, is my Higher Power. It is in this which is unnamable that I find the most authentic confidence. Knowing that it is our divine birthright to live our dreams offers me the *faith* and the *permission* to reach my tremendous potential. My ego is humbled by this knowledge and therefore my fear by the reminder *that I have a mission* while here on this Earth. I have a story to tell. I, like you, was put here *on* purpose *for* a purpose. And when you quiet your negative mental chatter to listen to your soul's messages, your courage muscle increases in strength and propels you towards your destiny. You will no longer struggle against fear because fear becomes your ally. You no longer fight with fear because it fuels you to strengthen your faith which boosts you into taking action. Remind yourself that y*our intuition gives you permission to access your greatness.* Remind yourself that it is your responsibility to do what your heart desires because your desires were placed there inside your heart when you were first introduced to this world. And remind yourself of this useful quote said by Marianne Williamson: "Our deepest fear is not that we are inadequate. Our deepest fear is that we are powerful beyond measure. It is our light, not our darkness, that most frightens us. You playing small does not serve the world."

Confront and release your fears by *befriending* them. In acknowledging your fears, you automatically minimize their potency. Develop and utilize personal, unique mantras to help you through the tough times. My favorite mantra is: "I will not allow fear to block my abundant blessings that await me." I hope these tools that I use every day will aid you in taking that next step so that you can share your gifts with the rest of the world making you a healthy and happy balanced mama.

Exercise: Facing fears to transform them into energy, passion, and drive

1) Fast forward your life. Imagine yourself 95 years old, about to transition. Listen to the message the man or

woman full of wisdom has to offer you—what did her

heart crave to do that fear stopped them from pursuing?

_____

_____

_____

_____

_____

2) Write and describe how *not* ever going after your dreams

caused more pain than the idea of failing at them.

_____

_____

_____

_____

_____

_____

3) Develop at least two powerful mantras to aid you in persisting through fear towards your goals.

_____

_____

_____

_____

_____

_____

Smile! Remember, you are on your path towards discovering your greatness! I don't know about you, but this *excites* me! Let's continue your journey of discovering your gifts; your greatness. This will all contribute to being a productive, happy mommy!

Let's close this chapter with a compelling speech by Theodore Roosevelt called the Man in the Arena which upon hearing last year changed my life forever and shifted my perception. After hearing this quote, I knew fear would never stop me from going after my dreams ever again.

"It is not the critic who counts; not the man who points out how the strong man stumbles, or where the doer of deeds could have done them better. The credit belongs to the man who is actually in the arena, whose face is marred by dust and sweat and blood; who strives valiantly; who errs, who comes short again and again, because there is no effort without error and shortcoming; but who does actually strive to do the deeds; who knows great enthusiasms, the great devotions; who spends himself in a worthy cause; who at the best knows in the end the triumph of high achievement, and who at the worst, if he fails, at least fails while daring greatly, so that his place shall never be with those cold and timid souls who neither know victory nor defeat."

What about you? What side do you feel more comfortable on? I know the only way I can be a happy, healthy mom is to go after the things I want most in life, even if going after those things scare me. I'd much rather be the woman *in* the arena getting her butt kicked from time to time, but who reaps the benefits of a life lived with direct intention, perseverance, inspiration, and authenticity. I decided not to care about the critics. Brene Brown is right, "Their opinions are *not* the ones who count".

Chapter 6

BENEFITS OF BEING AUTHENTIC & STAYING TRUE TO *YOU*

From the moment your mother birthed you into this amazing Universe, a very large portion of your personality was already predetermined. Psychologists refer to this genetic predisposition as our innate temperament. Your personality is similar to your fingerprint—astonishingly unique—no one else will share the exact copy you were given. It'd make little sense then to try and change or reject aspects of your personality which you may not understand that are so natural to yourself.

It can be incredibly relieving and invigorating to not only know, but to love and embrace exactly who you are meant to be. Embracing your gifts which come so naturally to you will inevitably result in higher productivity and happiness. You cannot accomplish what you truly want out of life without knowing who you are. Specifically, you cannot be a great mom if you are constantly in "soul searching mode" never really settling into the grove of who you are in the present moment. One thing you can benefit from related to embracing your authentic self is realizing that you are the *designed*, not the designer. You cannot change who you are, nor should you want to!

When I was younger, I covered up my true, gregarious spirit with that one of a shy, insecure one. Growing up the youngest girl of five children, I took on the role of the entertainer—the one who deflected and distracted people of our family's blatant dysfunction. I know that sounds a bit like an oxymoron—the fact that I was shy, yet entertaining—but allow me to further explain. I never felt I deserved a voice. Therefore, I rarely, if ever voiced an opinion. My siblings and parents grew comfortable with that. I chose another avenue of expression—performing. I danced, sang, and made others laugh. It was a great distraction for a while! But the repression grew too strong after a while and I realized I couldn't afford to live anyone else's personality by neglecting my own. ***Being inauthentic to your true nature can be especially taxing to your spirit.*** It dawned on me one day—life is far too short—I need to show the world who *I* am! The heck with this! I *am* outgoing, I love to talk, and I am opinionated—I *do* have a voice—hear me rooooaaaar!

That is what happens when you constantly suppress your true nature; you implode, explode, or a combination of the two—hence, my roaring. My mother to this day still tells me how shocked she is of my bold personality—"I thought you were always shy, Mo!" *Not really, mom, but— Nice to meet you too!*

I remember sitting in my teacher's office one afternoon when I was a senior about to graduate. Mr. Brown sat there and put a genuine effort into attempting to convince me to attend college. "College was the *best time of my life!*" he recollected with a huge smile. "How could you *not* want to go?" he asked, sincerely interested.

"Mmmm—college isn't for me," I said flatly in an uninspiring tone. College at the time did not seem appealing to me whatsoever. I didn't want to be like a lot of others I had witnessed—going to school for something in which I had no genuine interest for solely in hopes of making money to commit to a long life of doing what I lacked inspiration to do in the first place! While some are lucky and smart enough to get a degree in which they are gifted and passionate in—great! Unfortunately, this is not the case most of the time—rushing into adulthood and choosing a major and career prior to self-actualization can result in regret financially and soulfully. And that is what college wrongly represented to me at the time: a commonly traveled road to a fabricated, yet painfully unfulfilling success. I had no idea what I wanted to do with my life then. I did know on a soulful level, however, that I would **blaze my own trail to success** in whatever field I became passionate in. I somehow innately sensed that I knew I wouldn't reach my dreams via the road commonly traveled. Looking back, I wish I could've articulated this to Mr. Brown more effectively!

With that being said, later I did see the advantage of college—to learn! Going to college doesn't have to be all about making money and landing a career following graduation. This idea seems obvious, right?—go to school to learn for the sake and passion for learning—rather than going to school solely as a means to an end. Yet I see so many peers going to college to gain the approval and validation from parents and society—not because their authentic selves sense their degrees would enable them to share their gifts with the world. I can assure you won't enjoy your time chasing your degree if it is not purposeful. Be honest with yourself in regard to what you really want to do and axe out any naysaying thoughts such as, "I really want to be an artist, but I can't make any money in that field, so I'll settle for_____." The awesome news here is that when you follow your natural, intrinsic passion towards the career you love, money will inevitably follow.   However if you are chasing money and putting your authentic desires second, suffering and boredom will assuredly follow.   Many of my peers have admitted to me that their going to college was a means to get a job. Deep down I always knew that *I needed a dream, not a job.* I work to support myself and my family when financially necessary, of course, but ultimately my goal is to live a life of purpose by having a career I truly enjoy which includes sharing my gifts with the world and living my passion!

No one taught me the invaluable lesson growing up that *God blesses us with our own unique traits and packages them into gifts for us to share with the world*—I had to teach this to myself. I subconsciously bought into the defeating idea that we all needed to be the same; that we needed to conform to "make it" in life. What a load of hogwash! Are you telling me that the actual Creator of this magnificent Universe birthed each and every one of us completely unique by nature…on *accident?* Of course not! Hence we are urged to embrace our own individuality—urged to share our unique light with the world! We owe it not only to ourselves, but more importantly our Higher Power to fill the shoes He chose us to fill—regardless of whether or not *we* think they're too big. We wouldn't be given any mission here on Earth too grand, too beautiful, or too impossible.

And what a great legacy to leave to your family—the value of serving the world via authentic self-expression. I want my son to know that one of his mother's most prized values is the gift of being true to whom you really are life. We were all blessed with unique gifts so that we can fulfill the job we were chosen to fulfill while here on this Earth. So— be yourself! Be confident and courageous! Embrace your quirkiness—embrace everything about you with the grace that you know *God made no one else in this entire Universe with the combination of your strengths, talents, and personality.* More importantly, if *you* do not share your gifts in this life, who will? The potential of giving birth to your creative ideas will forever be gone if you do not accept responsibility in your life to share them.

I sigh and smile as I think of how incredibly relieving it is to be happy with being myself. I could've saved many hours of many days from being depressed years ago if I knew that it was *okay to be me.* But that is alright—it was not wasted time—it was all a part of my journey towards self-actualization.

If you do not take the time to discover you—to define yourself in this life, others will. And it can be incredibly crippling to your self-esteem if you willingly give your power away to others by *allowing them* to define *you.* I want my children to know who they are so that they can walk tall into any situation in life and never allow anyone to cause them to shrink their personality due to feelings of unjust inferiority. The best way to create this foundation for your kids is to master the art of owning who *you* are as a parent. Know that your kids will learn from you by your *example* and not by your preaching.

So, how do you find out you really are, anyway?

If you are unsure of where to start and you need a little push in a guided direction, there is a very easy, useful tool in becoming aware of your personality—the Myers-Briggs personality test. It is a personality assessment created by Isabel Myers Briggs based off famous psychologist Carl Jung's research. I was first introduced to this test when I was a sophomore in college taking a nonverbal communication course. Our homework assignment was to complete the test and write a three page response on our reaction to the results. I took the test three times in a row—it was fun! Each time, I'd remind myself to answer the questions as *honestly as possible* to better ensure accuracy of results. For the past four years—

I've always scored as an ENFP—Extroverted, Intuition, Feeling, Perceiving. I suggest hopping on the internet and going to humanmetrics.com to complete your free assessment. On that site you can find any additional answers you may be seeking concerning the test. When my children are of an appropriate age, I'll definitely have them do this test as well! It is fun and informative.

It may seem over-simplistic, but seeing a gist of your personality on paper will be liberating, inspiring, and reassuring. With the new knowledge I gained once completing this test, I was better able to understand *why* my secretarial job was so uninspiring to me, while my colleagues seemed perfectly content within their position, and why the single thought of filing paperwork made my skin crawl with dread. (While I was supposed to put away documents, I'd frequently get caught dancing in the filing room to wake my spirits up!) In short, the office scene is not meant for my personality type. You will be much more useful to uplifting the world if you are in a career that correlates with your talents and gifts.

We all naturally acquire strengths and weaknesses and it is incredibly empowering to learn of your own so you can be drawn towards careers and lifestyles genuinely appealing to your unique temperament. What this test did for me was offer me a glimpse into my true gifts that would ultimately lead me towards my destiny. Once you understand your genuine temperament, you can thereby begin searching for careers by which you are authentically aligned. The world would be such a better place if we all had careers which were aligned with our values and temperaments.

Personality tests are just the tip of the iceberg. Something a bit more profound is required to find yourself— and that activity is soul searching. Soul searching is essential in ensuring you are living the life you are meant to be living by being on the path you are meant to be on.

This process of self-actualization is not always a one-stop shop. At times it will require trying on of different outfits or careers in life to see which one fits your unique spirit. Soul searching for me included much *trial and error.* I tried on different lifestyles to see which one felt right. I tried the outfit of modeling on for a couple of years—I even landed a spot in Maxim—yet this role did not feel appropriate to my authentic self. I knew I had to move on. Here it is important to note that flexibility will be of high value concerning finding your purpose.

I danced in music videos and pursued countless dance projects from doing a tour to performing in plays. I even go-go danced at one of New Mexico's hottest clubs. And while dancing is a gift of mine, I always felt like I was missing out on something larger when dancing for an audience of attendees. I wanted to *talk* to audiences and inspire them, yet I felt confined with my role to solely use my body (and not my mind) for other's entertainment and appeasement. I thought that since dancing was a natural gift of mine that the dancing limelight had to be my destiny, but as it turns out dancing under strobe lights and on top of stages was only a *chapter* in my life. It wasn't until I gave birth to my son at age 26 that I realized performing via dancing on a stage wasn't any longer my life's primary calling. A different plan or path for my life was being drawn to me and I was okay with that! My heart began to yearn for connection with audiences in a different way that *was congruent with the woman I was becoming, not the woman I had been.* With this understanding I hung up my modeling and dance costumes switching them with my new outfit—public speaking, writing, and fitness coaching.

Coming to terms and being excited about my newfound purpose was exhilarating, but came at the price of a bit of wasted resources. At first, I was stubborn and went about finding my destiny my way, and ended up trying on other folks' shoes so to speak! If my friend whom I may have respected seemed content in a 9-5 and urged me to do the same, I would try on her outfit or lifestyle in hopes of feeling some closure. Of course, following another on *their* path never works! Sometimes, we look at a friend—how *she* lives, what *her* spiritual beliefs are, how *she* supports her family—and you try on her role for *your* life! Yet we will never attain happiness, health, and emotional fulfillment if we are busy copying someone else's idea of success.

Have you ever done that—tried on a shoe you knew didn't fit, but bought them and wore them anyway because they were just so cute? Many of us, like me, are guilty of doing this literally and figuratively. My efforts did not go in vain, however. I learned a valuable lesson: While it is better to try *something* rather than to stay in your comfort zone, *make sure the attempt is genuine to your true spirit.* Forced passion is not true passion.

I began listening to my own inner wisdom, my intuition, to help guide me towards the right goals in tune with my own unique spirit. And what I discovered was that I was able to avoid a lot of unnecessary pain when doing just that.

When you are aligned, conscious and aware of your own potential and gifts in life, you will begin to attract all the right people and circumstances that will help propel you towards your happiest life. When you're busy trying on someone else's version of a happy life, though, you stunt your own growth, cutting off all potential for true happiness.

One of the best values you can pass on to your children is the gift of being true to yourself in life. If your child is naturally gregarious, celebrate this by refraining from any criticism of his outgoing personality. On the other hand, if your child is naturally introverted, allow and encourage her quiet time needed to do activities such as reading or journaling.

When you know who you are and what you value, it makes making decisions so much easier in life. I now know to look within the depths of my own heart to find answers to my burning questions in life—should I move? Should I take the job? Should I stay in this relationship?

When I was younger, I expected others to validate my heart's answers by instructing me of what *they* thought I should do next. While I do still appreciate the wisdom from others whom I admire from time to time, I know I can rely on my own inner guidance system to make decisions (more on intuition in the next chapter.) When I finally owned my own intuitive power, I was able to finally own my future and claim my power. And how empowering is that?

When you learn to rejoice in who you are not only as a mom but as the woman you are destined to be, you are in effect teaching your children that they too can do the same. The more you allow yourself to shine by honoring your true self, the more others will find permission to allow themselves to shine in life in their own special way.

Exercise: Staying true to your authentic nature

1) Complete the Myers-Briggs test online at humanmetrics.com. Do the results coincide with who you view yourself to be? Why or why not?

_____

_____

_____

_____

_____

2) Think of an example when you knew you were going against your true nature. What physical/emotional sensations caused you to be aware of this? (Example: You were in a job you despised—what feelings did you have internally to make you aware that you were not in the right predicament?)

_____

_____

_____

_____

_____

_____

3) What did you really value doing as a child between the ages of 4-13? These hobbies offer major clues as to who you are meant to become as an adult.

_____

_____

_____

_____

_____

_____

Chapter 7

HONOR YOUR INTUITION & ABUNDANCE WILL FOLLOW

The single best day of my entire life was the day I gave birth to my beautiful son, Eliel. That divine Monday morning, my labor proceeded with seemingly little to no effort, and within hours I met my baby boy after carrying him those 10 months in excited anticipation. I couldn't believe God blessed me with this amazing gift—the gift of being able to carry life. Abundant gratitude filled my heart as I looked into Eliel's eyes for the first time. I knew my life had been forever changed and for the better.

During my pregnancy, labor and delivery, I reflected on past, present and images of my future. I felt overwhelmingly grateful for the opportunity to be a mom— to give a new soul in this life a fresh start.

The morning Eliel was born, I cried and laughed and sighed as I stared at my son for the first time. I tuned everyone else out present in the room—the nurses, my mom—in my head it was just my son, my husband, and God there in the room that sunny morning. The day I gave birth was the day I realized *anything was possible.* Becoming a mom that beautiful morning was my moment of being in the Universal Presence of Abundant Flow. With sunrays streaming in my delivery room on November 12, 2012, I felt the overwhelming, yet silent presence of my Higher Power, and I was thankful for the opportunity to be a receiver of such a special gift. I knew that regardless of any fear I had about becoming a parent my heart's intuition had guided us towards our best and most abundant life. I knew I had made the right choice to start a family.

Who knows if I would have ever seen this miraculous life changing moment if I'd listened to others' advice? Many well-meaning (and single) friends warned us: *Enjoy your* *marriage longer! Kids suck the energy right outta you! Focus on your business and then plan for a baby. Save up $10,000 first!* Your friends and relatives can mean well and have the best intentions for you when offering advice concerning the future of your life, but ultimately it is up to *you* to listen to *your* heart to truly know when what is best in order to be a receiver of an abundant life.

Through meditation, I had already been offered a glimpse of what life would be like pregnant and in love with my husband before it actually happened in real life and came into fruition. I saw sweet images of Elvis rubbing my belly, telling me how beautiful I was and speaking to my large tummy, explaining to our son, Eliel, how he couldn't wait to meet him. That was followed with mental pictures of Elvis and I taking our son to the park, zoo, and throwing him birthday parties. I sat there sitting Indian style meditating on these images that flowed effortlessly into consciousness months before conceiving our firstborn. Tears fell down my cheeks as I smiled—I knew God had planted those images in my head and heart on purpose—without that seed planted that day through meditation I wouldn't have been able to even fathom the potentiality of growing such a sweet, loving, and tender life for my family. Sometimes when Elvis, Eliel and I are at the park having the family time I used to see mental images of in the past, I stop in awe and gratitude of my life. I acknowledge the Universe for helping to co-create the amazing life I now have I that I only used to dream about.

You have to allow yourself to get comfortable with your dreams in life—no matter how big, unique or impossible they may seem and regardless of the amount of fear that may want to keep you from moving forward. You must allow yourself to become comfortable in the presence of your authentic desires. Whether you want to adopt a baby, move to France, or start your own business you must give yourself permission to envision images of the future living the dreams you desire to manifest. When you have a vision of what your life could look like handed down by your Higher Power and realize in affirmation the *divinity* of your dreams, *no one* will have the power to talk you out of your dreams! The surefire way of knowing if your dreams are truly meant for your life to manifest is by noticing if the thought of doing that something moves you to tears. If so, you know you are in the presence of your inner guidance; that which is illogical yet moves mountains in your spirit. It is your job to obey your heart's orders once you know them. Doing this will always result in a more fulfilling, happy, and abundant life.

As I stated in Chapter 5, I was terrified about opening up Elvis and my first restaurant, Pasión Latin Fusion. Yet, I was able to move and work past the fear once I quieted my loud, fearful thoughts. My intuition told me I was safe to move forward and that my family would be supported in our business endeavors. And of course, the Universe never lies. Pasión is succeeding beyond our wildest dreams.   Our journey of being restaurant owners has been difficult at times and I did want to quit when some days seemed like too much. But one day my intuition tapped me on the shoulder and guided me to apply for the hit Food Network show, Restaurant: Impossible. It took hours and days to finish the application, and at one point the application was erased and I had to start from scratch. I continued the process despite my logic trying to convince me my efforts were in vain. And one day about 3 months later, I unexpectedly received a phone call from the show's producers. Even though she confided that our chances of being chosen for the show were still relatively low, and that I "shouldn't get my hopes too high", I knew it was a wrap. I knew we'd be chosen. I can't explain it in any other way than feeling like sharing our story with the world was meant to be—like the Universe had orchestrated the events to unfold in the most beneficial way if I proceeded with faithful intuition.

Being on Restaurant: Impossible was a surreal

experience and one that I will always hold dear to my heart. My desire in life is to inspire others with my story, my authenticity, and my revelations. I knew being on Restaurant: Impossible was meant to be. I understand this retrospectively because like my job in HR, I didn't have the guts to quit my role as manager, so I had to be fired. That is exactly what Chef Irvine did—released me from my position as manager of my own business—and I thank him! My addiction to being manager of the front of house was a negative attachment—my talents were needed in other areas of life for which I was so much better suited. But I ignored my intuition and thought it was my duty to help my husband and my business by being overworked and ultimately growing resentful due to this fact. It was too much—I was also taking full time classes, managing my blog, and was a full time mommy. What my heart truly wanted was to gather some courage to go after my own dreams while being able to care for my son, but I was afraid of failing so I clung to my husband's dream (Pasión), even though it felt like I was wearing someone else's outfit or career. And this is the gift being on the show taught me: *If you are unwilling to listen to the guidance and follow signs for your life, you will be forced to.* I don't think I'll ever need to be fired from another position to understand this fact. I'm going to pay attention to my intuition and gut feelings and stick to roles that are aligned with my gifts and talents so that I am contributing the best me to this world! In short, remember this: The Universe basically can force you to go after your life's purpose if you don't have the initiative to do so yourself.

Who says you have to "play it safe" by choosing careers or lifestyles that are uninspiring to you? Whoever does, kick them to the curb! Surround yourself with those whom are supportive, loving, and when required, a little *unrealistic.* Relinquish the outdated belief that you have to be "adult" by choosing uninspiring yet affluent careers and succumb to mediocrity in any facet of your life because it's just not true!

I remember sitting at a friend's dinner party a few years back before opening Pasión Latin Fusion. I sat there with a cold glass of chardonnay in my hand, talking with my friend Jordan. "Jordan, I just can't figure out what to major in—any advice?" I was a sophomore in college and felt really pressured to decide. He leaned in. "Mo, I think it's about time you grow up and pick a major that is in demand— something that can get you a decent paying job like computers or something in a hospital." Jordan said in a serious tone. *Hmmm,* I thought. *He makes a decent point. What's in demand? Nursing!—Oh, wait, I can't stand the sight of blood. Engineering!—wait, math is not my forte. Information Technology?—definitely not for my personality type.*

Looking back, I could've saved years of agonizing indecision by simply following my heart. But I fought my intuition because it seemed... illogical (Hint: intuition is rarely 'logical'). I thought something was severely wrong with me! I looked around as seemingly everyone else was choosing majors, graduating from college, and starting their careers. I just couldn't figure out why *deciding* who I wanted to be and what I wanted to do was so difficult for me. One day I'd wake up and proclaim—"I'm gonna be a paralegal!" It wasn't my passion, but I was pretty confident I could find a job after graduation. But next month I'd change my mind—"I'm gonna major in journalism!—I could be a news caster!" No…that didn't feel quite right either. What my heart truly wanted to do was to *inspire* people with my life's story…to be an entrepreneur. To be my *own* boss! But I was afraid to act on those desires because I didn't feel worthy. And the chatter commenced: *Who—lil' ole me? The black and Puerto Rican girl raised in poverty on the south side of Chicago—be someone's boss? No, you must have the wrong girl! I'm not good enough for that!*

So, I suffered. You see, when you fight God's plan for you, when you fight your intuition—what you *know* you should do—you're bound to be depressed. If you want to feel alive and joyful in this life, I suggest that you grab your cojones and go after what your soul desires regardless of the lack of rationale. Be bold enough to be honest with yourself. Be bold enough to go after your dreams.

Being an entrepreneur has always been in my blood. So it feels natural; it feels right. I remember when I was 10 years old—3rd grade to be exact. I'd save up all my allowances and I would invest it. You may laugh, but hear me out. I would walk across this large field right outside our apartment—it was a shortcut—to the Hostess Bakery store. I'd walk in the store, buy packages of Twinkies, cupcakes, and pies at a mere 33 cents a pop. Then I'd walk all the way back; back across that same field, but this time I wouldn't go home. I would walk around my neighborhood, knocking on doors, selling my baked goodies at an inflated price of one dollar. I would make a 57 cents profit each cake. Multiply that by thirty cakes—that's about an $18 profit in thirty minutes. And when you are a kid raised in poverty, that's a lot of money.

I share this story with you to remind you that *childhood hobbies offer clues as to what we're destined to do—who we're destined to become.* There's something completely fearless inside the spirit of a child. When we're kids, we feel as though we can do anything we want to do. Why is this? I believe it has to do with the fact that no one's told us otherwise yet! It's when we become adults that our life views become narrowed and confined. It's when we become adults that we start to think too *realistically*.

Some people, like my friend Jordan, oppose this idea that we can do what our natural gifts call us to do with the notion that one should be *realistic* and methodical. What a depressing, confining term, *realistic*. Why would anyone ever want to settle for being realistic? There is a negative connotation covertly attached to this idea. Being realistic can be synonymous with being practical or logical which are potentially equally boring ideas. Psychologists who have done studies on optimism will tell you that *pessimists* tend to be the most realistic. Will Smith once said that, "Being realistic is the most commonly traveled road to mediocrity", and I believe he is right. If you don't mind living a life of mediocrity, then play it safe! Put down this book! Keep the 9-5 no matter how much your heart is begging you do to otherwise. Stay in that unfulfilling relationship. Don't work out—you're right—it *is* too hard! But remember this: Your life is your message to the world. I don't know about you, but I want to make mine inspiring. And if you're compelled to keep reading, then I think you do too.

Do you believe you're worthy of a life filled with abundance? A very liberating moment came to me the moment I truly understood that the Universe overflowed with abundance and that ***abundance was available to all.*** The first step in retrieving abundance is realizing that it is *there.* Want a more inspiring career? It's possible. Want more fulfilling relationships? A nicer house? A better body? It's possible! Society, our upbringing and the media can send out subtle messages conflicting with this idea, as though happiness and success is only available to a predetermined select few—wrong! Greatness is available to *anyone with the courage to grab it.* They never taught us how to be the person we're destined to be in school though. That, my friends, is up to us. Seemingly the most valuable, priceless knowledge we can retrieve on this Earth is learned internally, guided with a higher wisdom—wisdom connected to our intuition.

I remember growing up with an incredibly narrow view of life's abundances. We were often evicted from apartments, homeless, and only bought a "new car" when our current lemon broke down. At a very young age, I subconsciously developed the idea that more affluent, happier people lived over *there.* I believed that resources like good food, good education, and beautiful homes existed, but I succumbed to the notion that *those things weren't available for kids like me.* When I was younger, around the time I started selling those hostess cakes, I knew I would create a better life for myself when I grew up—a life that represented abundance, not poverty—both externally and internally. Don't get me wrong, our family made the most out of our circumstances, but I always knew that I wanted more.

It wasn't until I realized I *could* dream bigger that I *began to allow myself* to dream bigger. By the time I graduated from high school I realized living paycheck to paycheck with an uninspiring job didn't have to be my reality. It suddenly dawned on me that I, too, could be a homeowner, even if I never had that opportunity growing up. I, too, could be a successful business woman! I, too, could live an abundant life!

No one is telling us that we cannot do what our hearts desire; that we cannot accomplish our dreams because they seem impossible. So why would we ever settle for anything less than a life of abundance? It can be quite the relief to let go of any limiting beliefs that may have been fed to you while growing up subconsciously. Paying close attention to how self-limiting messages from your childhood may be creeping into your subconscious now will be helpful in this process of accepting abundance as not only adults, but as parents.

How are you supposed to quiet your obnoxiously loud thoughts to hear your intuition which will lead you towards your happiest and healthiest life? Well, for me, exercising—jogging in nature or dancing—helps me clear my head to hear my heart. Journaling, reading, and spending time alone also helps me recharge with divine inspiration. I strongly urge you to discover *what connects you to the Universal Spirit*. For some, religion, yoga, meditation, or even conversing with a close friend can do the trick. Whatever it is, go deep! Go deep within yourself to find the answers to your own burning questions. It is within your own heart that you will find the guidance for what *you* need to do to take the first steps toward the life you want. I recommend listening to your whispers of your heart *before* they turn into knocks. Why wait until life smacks you in the face? Have the courage to answer's life's knocks *before* you are in desperation.

You, too, can partner with your intuition, or your inner GPS system, to make you the happiest, most healthy mom you know. What is your heart guiding you to do? Often, I find that when I am in meditation, I will have strong urges guiding me towards a decision, but my head won't be on board. Logic and intuition are old school enemies, they never really got along. But you can outsmart this duo by choosing to honor your heart's calling while simultaneously doing so in a methodical way. When you do choose to honor your intuition more so than your head or surface desires, more opportunities will arise to support your calling leading you towards a life of abundance. The Universe will open up doors that were previously unopened. You will be provided with the opportunities that are aligned with your purpose and gifts which will ultimately lead to the life of your dreams. The Universe is overflowing with abundance—the Universe is just waiting on us to have the faith to go after what you want—what your hearts desires—to believe it's possible!

Exercise: Attracting the lives we really want

1) Think of a time when you followed your intuition— your gut feeling—and you were rewarded. How did you feel during this time? What cues did your body offer you that guided you towards this correct decision/move? The idea probably seemed illogical, but it felt right. What did that feel like? Most likely, you felt an overwhelming feeling in your solar plexus that was difficult to ignore. If so or not, what else?

_____

_____

_____

_____

_____

_____

_____

2)   Take the time to write down and design the life of your dreams. What does it look like? Who do you look life? Where do you live? What are you doing, and who is sharing the journey with you? Get specific.

_____

_____

_____

_____

_____

_____

_____

3)   Describe at least three reasons why you are worthy of abundance.

_____

_____

_____

_____

_____

_____

4) What has your intuition been guiding you to do that you may have been conveniently ignoring? Be honest and specific!

_____

_____

_____

_____

_____

_____

_____

The next time you need a reminder of overflowing

abundance, remember this metaphor: Picture everyone walking down a crowded street. There is a pot of gold sitting there on the side, right next to a big tree on the sidewalk. People pass right on by the pot of gold. Some eye it with feelings of envy, while others don't even dare to glare in its direction. For about every *18,000* people that pass, *one person* has the courage to dip their hands in the gold. Others witness saying, "Oh, how lucky she/he is to get some gold...!" But what is stopping *them*? Fear? Indolence? Lack of self-confidence? Lack of faith? Whatever it may be— decide *now* that you will no longer watch on the sidelines as others redeem their blessings in life! Decide that you are worthy of abundance in your life.

Chapter 8

BRINGING IT ALL TOGETHER TO BE A HEALTHY, HAPPY MOMMY

I would like to begin closing this book by saying "We teach that which we need most". I first heard this quote—initially said by Rich Bach—while driving home one sunny day in Albuquerque with my three month old son. We were tuning in to one of Leslie Brown's inspiring speeches on my iPod. Once I heard this quote, I subtly realized my destiny.

You see I've always been an active and willing student in this roller coaster ride called life. And for a long time I've been *obsessed* with learning all things genuinely self-helping, motivating, and life transforming—I knew at a young age that I needed these things to keep me grounded on the right path in life.

I'll be the first to admit unapologetically that sometimes I can still be a *hot mess*. Lauryn Hill once said that she works every day at becoming *less* of a hot mess. The difference between the younger version of myself and the woman I am today is that I don't stay there—I don't remain in the city called Hot-Messville. I've developed these tools outlined in this book to help me through days that are far from perfect. There is not one person on this entire globe who escapes the reality that they too experience not so fun moments of fear, confusion, anger, and so on at some point in their lives. We will never have it all together *all* the time. What we choose to do with these damaging emotions is the determining factor in how we live our lives. One who chooses to stew in the pot of soup called fear is choosing to delay their own imperative inner healing. One who chooses to bask in the ocean called anger is choosing to defer living a life full of love and abundance. And one who chooses to lie in the hammock of self-hatred is only suspending the beautiful horizon of self-love. And I don't know about you but I want to pass on a legacy of self-love, appreciation, and healing to my kids. And how do I do that? By living each day purposefully and by being a healthy, happy mom!

Even the most talented and wise spiritual teachers of today still experience feelings of self-doubt, fear, and at times lack the self-love and appreciation necessary to get whatever task at hand done effectively. In other words, we are never "done" with our spiritual growth. But ever since I was tapped on the shoulder one evening and informed that I had a mission to spread love, light and truth, *I surrendered.* I decided to relinquish all motivation of selfish gain to pave a way for a purposeful life. I knew one of my missions while here was to show other women that it is possible to have a happy, healthy, well-balanced life. And although I am 100% certain I was chosen to write this book and eventually become a spiritual teacher, I, of course, at times still experience doubt and low self-esteem. This book is one *I* continuously reference back to when experiencing feelings of doubt or fear—when I lack the faith necessary to propel my life to the next level.

So this is not some pompous book that puts me on top of the mountain and you in a mole hill.   When starting out writing this book, it was to serve as a reminder for me—I needed a valuable set of tools to *equip* me mentally and spiritually so that I could begin to live my life filled with intense meaning, purpose, and love.   Being granted me countless visions of what my life could potentially entail if I began living the life I was destined to live, I finally mustered up the courage to live unapologetically towards my dreams. And so this book serves as a declaration and compilation of the mental and emotional obstacles placed in my own path, and how I managed to remove them to move forward with confidence and to be a healthy, happy mom while doing just that!

It's our challenges in life that unites us—that reminds us we are all the same—we're all human.   We all crave happiness and want to avoid pain. Yet we all experience both emotions consistently—that is just life. Yet, there's always a hidden gem lying in our darkest moments: We always come out stronger, wiser, and more spiritually aware when we climb out of the dark holes of despair and hurt. I have learned the most thus far in my life *through climbing out of the holes of my darkest days*. What's been reassuring for me is the fact that there has always been a rainbow of wisdom waiting for me on the opposite side. So when potential clients bluntly ask me what makes me "qualified" to help guide them in changing their lives, I smile and respond, "My struggle". If the tools created and listed in this book can assist me with getting through tough times, then I can be confident they can help you too.

I am not here to lie and pretend that changing your perceptions, your outlook or your life is easy. But I *am* here to remind you that it is more than *possible*. It is my humble hope that you feel more loved, joyful, and free after reading this book.

Life is about living passionately and healthily with love and abundance. That is how we are able to wake up every day grateful to be alive! God has blessed us with a body to live and experience *joy* in this life—let's not waste another day away!

The end of this book is only the beginning—what are *you* willing to do today that will bring you closer to a higher vision for your life? You've already been blessed with an awesome set of unique talents called *gifts*—are you willing to utilize them for a cause bigger than yourself and diminish selfish motivation to serve the world? What are you willing to do that you've never done before that is out your comfort zone to get you there? What are you willing to *risk* to *become* the woman, the mommy of your dreams? The world is waiting for you to show us who you are—to share with us your gifts!

The image I hold in my head of the 'me I can be' is an

inspiring one. I want to continue to grow into a more loving, more joyful, more God serving individual with each day passing while simultaneously remaining content and humble. I want to do it for my Higher Power, myself, my son Eliel, husband Elvis, and everyone else I share my life with including *you*. I promise myself and all of you that I will continue to discover the gifts given to me, nurture them, and bring them into fruition. I believe this is our job once we are put on this Earth—to live our mission. It is through living my passion that pure inspiration will flow through my heart, connecting me to the Source. This is how we can be one of the happiest, healthy mommies we know!

Exercise: Tying it all together

1) What do you promise yourself that you will change about your life—*right now* to submit to an even better version of yourself? (Do you have any addictions? Do you need to

make a phone call, mend a relationship, or even start taking better care of your health?)

_____

_____

_____

_____

_____

_____

A) When you lack the strength to share your gifts, list at least two individuals who you do not wish to disappoint that will foster strength in your heart to move forward when you are tired, insecure, and are lacking faith. (For me, this is my son, my husband, and you!)

_____

_____

_____

_____

_____

_____

2) Write a letter to your children (born or not yet born). Let them know what your most prized values are. Do you value an incredible work ethic, a good heart, altruism? Get clear and write your personal values down so you can pass your legacy on to your family.

_____

_____

_____

_____

_____

_____

_____

_____

_____

_____

_____

3) Create a plan of how you envision your life—how you want it to look in the next year. Include any and all areas that call to your heart—career, family, health and spirituality. Make an action plan that is going to get you there—be flexible when coming up with the means. As my mom says, "There's more than one way to skin a cat".

_____

_____

_____

_____

_____

_____

_____

_____

_____

_____

_____

_____

4) Develop 4 compelling reasons why you are worthy of making these radical shifts in your life. (Example: I am worthy of making these changes because I deserve to live at my highest potential.)

_____

_____

_____

_____

_____

_____

5) How did becoming a mommy change you for the better? What activity can you start today to feel like an even better mom? (Example: Take your family to the park. Cook a nutritious meal. Read to your toddler.)

_____

_____

_____

_____

_____

_____

_____

_____

_____

You've sat on the sidelines of life long enough. It's time to reach up, reach out, and grab *your* blessings. It's time to introduce the world to the giant within *you*. It is time to clean up our act so that you can be the woman you are meant to be. We will be ready to greet you with love, acceptance, and appreciation *as soon as you are ready*. So, what are you waiting for? Nurture yourself unapologetically. Get your best body. Detox your life. Dare to dream big. Smack fear right in the face. Stay true to yourself. Honor your intuition and abundance *will* follow. These are the 7 habits that have made me one of the healthiest, happiest moms I know. I invite you implement these habits as they will undoubtedly do the same for you!

All of our dreams are one; connected by loving, endless energy. Follow your desires, for they offer the keys to your destiny. Dare to dream bigger for your life than you were taught to—be the biggest dreamer of anyone you know! Doing so is setting the best possible example for not only your children, but all your lives affects. Trust, believe, do the work, and you'll see—you will be smiled down upon and your life will be showered with unlimited abundance.

Let's all develop the habits of healthy, happy moms and apply all the tools learned in this book diligently and passionately today! Your kids will thank you in the best way—by growing up and blossoming into healthy, happy adults themselves.

BOOK BONUS:

Blog post on www.MomsWearHeels.com

WHY BEING A MOMMY ROCKS

Being a mommy is the hardest job I've ever had, yet ironically, the most joyful and fulfilling work I've ever done. Being responsible for another little person's well-being, safety, and health may seem daunting to most, and I do not judge anyone for their decisions to not procreate (It ain't my business!) Rather, what I can do is share my experiences with you all and hope that I can offer some companionship, inspiration, or understanding to some fellow moms and moms-to-be!

After becoming a mommy, I began to realize I'm a bit more old school than I'd like to admit. I love and thrive when I'm cooking breakfast for my husband, rocking my baby boy to sleep, and performing other wifey-mommy duties.

As soon as I had my son, I knew I wanted to have more kids. Thankfully, Elvis agrees. I used to chuckle in disbelief when other women mentioned wanting 3, 4, or even 5 kids, but now I'm actually beginning to understand their desire!

This confession is not to say that I will or want to have 5 kids. Instead, consider it an ode to moms everywhere. Below are my reasons to date why I love being a mom:

Why I love being a mommy:

1. Being pregnant was the most beautiful, natural chapter of my life (sans the hormonal acne :/)

2. Feeling my boy kick when in the Movie Theater for the first time brought sheer excitement and joy to my heart like no other!

3. Giving birth was the **best** experience of my life. Wouldn't trade it for the world.

4. Bringing my son home from the hospital felt like I'd won the lottery. (*Really*? You mean, I get to *keep* him??)

5. Breastfeeding: ultimate bonding experience

6. Seeing Elvis and myself in another human being we created out of pure love: priceless

7. Cuddling with Eliel to sleep: Heaven

8. Seeing a first tooth, second tooth, or fifth tooth feels like the first time.

9. His smile! My boy's smile melts away any anxiety or fear I may have been feeling.

10. Eliel has sparked Divine Inspiration within me now more than ever; forgiving others, letting go of toxic people and activities--so much easier now that I have him to set an example for.

11. He's so darn cute. (All moms should think their child is the most adorable).

12. Making him a green smoothie (with formula, or breast milk, spinach, and berries) and watching him gobble it down made me so proud! #healthybaby

13. Seeing Elvis and his son bond and play: priceless. Makes me fall in love with Elvis that much more

14. Crawling around on floor and making my son LOL; more pricelessness

15. Looking forward to all the milestones!

16. Experiencing the milestones!

17. The gift of being able to start family traditions; every Sunday is a full day of family time.

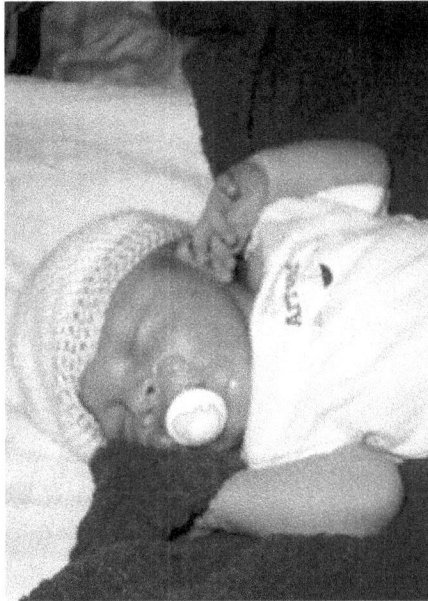

18. When we brought him home from the hospital! Really did feel like I'd won the lotto ☺

Those are some of the reasons I love being a mommy!

Why do *you* love being a mommy? Write down your reasons below:

1. _____

2. _____

3. _____

4. _____

5. _____

6. _____

7. _____

8. _____

9. _____

Check out www.MomsWearHeels.com   for even more current updates to be a happy, healthy mom!

For visual inspiration including recipes, fitness workouts, and more of Monica's daily life, follow her on http://instagram.com/fitmom118.

For awesome fitness videos, subscribe to Monica's page at http://www.youtube.com/monicabencomo.

And for all you twitter folks, follow here: https://twitter.com/MonicaBencomo18.

And if you are ever in the Albuquerque area, visit me at our restaurant Pasión Latin Fusion. www.pasionlatinfusion.com

www.ingramcontent.com/pod-product-compliance
Lightning Source LLC
Chambersburg PA
CBHW061946070426
42450CB00007BA/1071